LITTLE LESSONS

For Brian, Kyle, and Jacob.

For information about permission to reproduce
selections from this book, please contact
permissions@astrapublishinghouse.com.

mineditionUS

An imprint of Astra Books for Young Readers,
a division of Astra Publishing House
astrapublishinghouse.com

Printed in China

ISBN: 978-1-6626-5117-5 (hc)
ISBN: 978-1-6626-5118-2 (eBook)
Library of Congress Control Number: 2022901200

First edition
10 9 8 7 6 5 4 3 2 1

Illustration and design by Seymour Chwast
Associate design by Camille Murphy
The text is hand-lettered by Seymour Chwast
and set in his typeface Baseball.
The illustrations are done in pen and ink
on paper with digital color.

LITTLE LESSONS

SEYMOUR CHWAST

mineditionUS

OF A TREE.

A LEOPARD CANNOT CHANGE ITS SPOTS.

MANY
HANDS
MAKE
LIGHT
WORK.

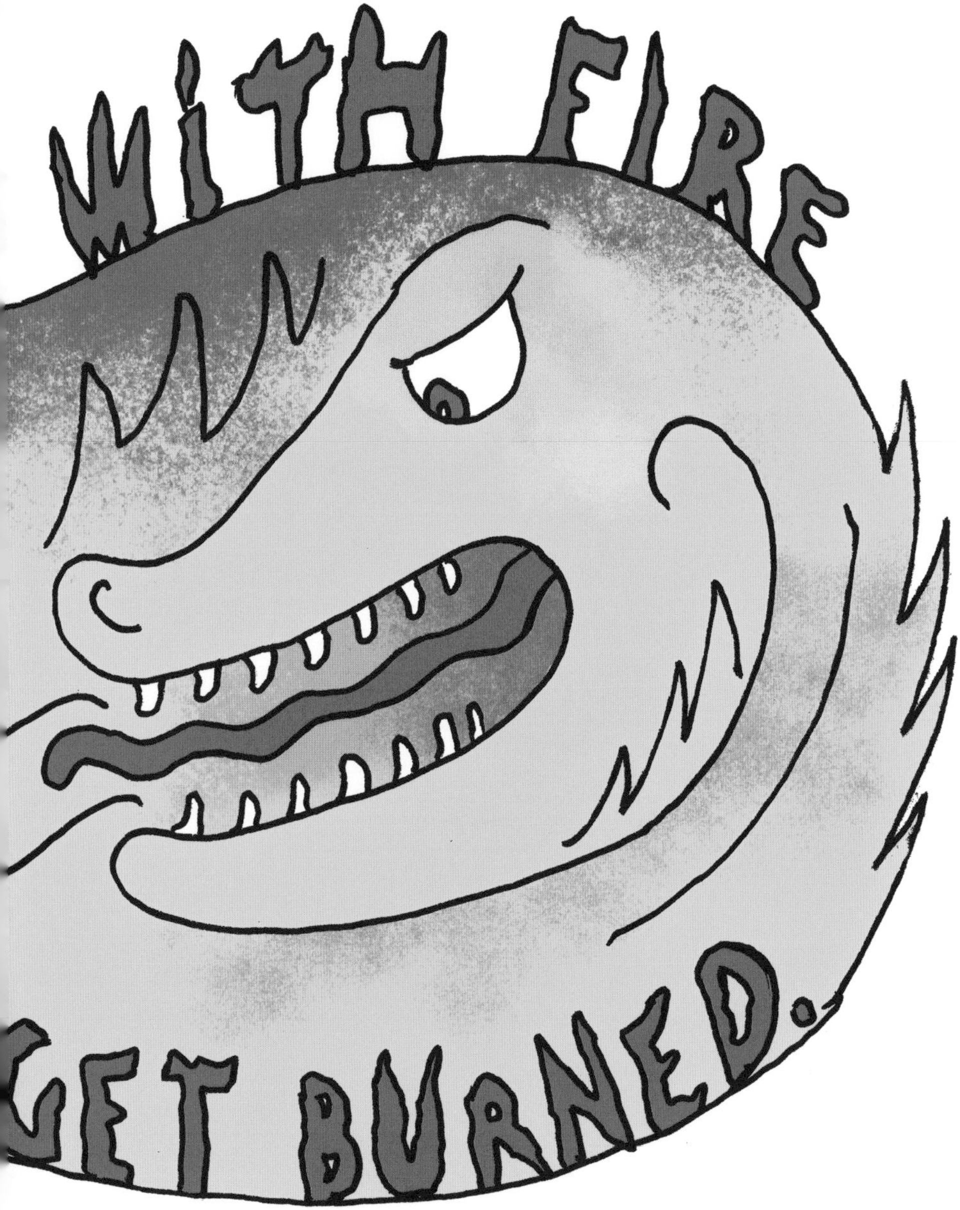
WITH FIRE
GET BURNED.

DON'T BITE OFF MORE THAN YOU CAN CHEW.

A BAD CARPENTER BLAMES HIS TOOLS.

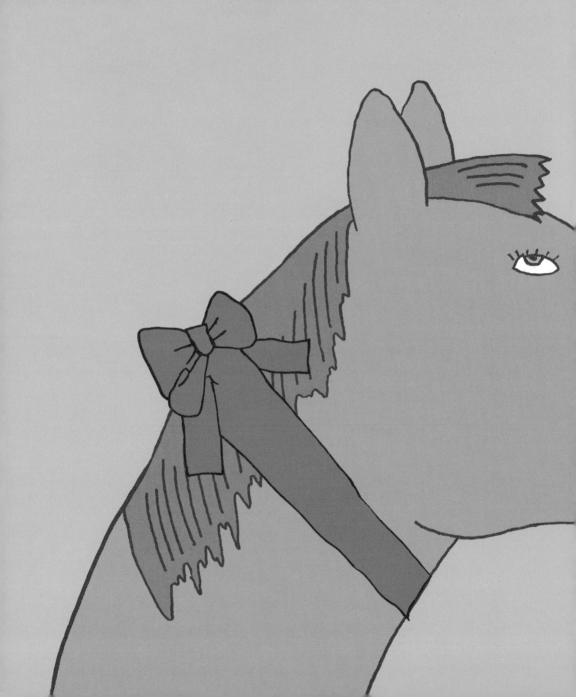

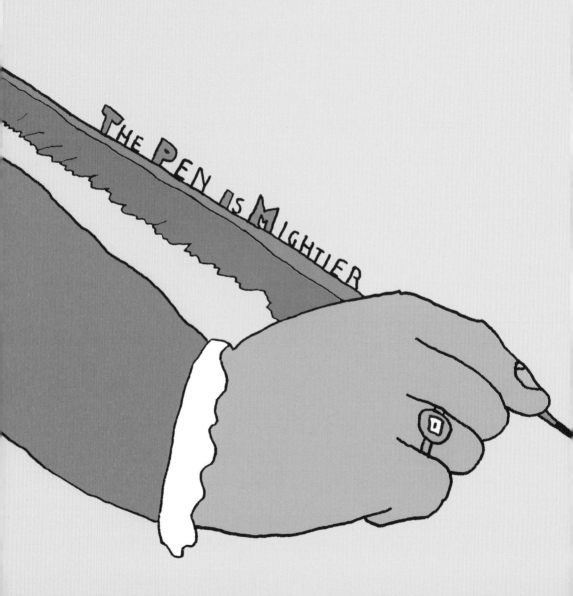

WHEN A MOUSE LAUGHS
AT A CAT
THERE IS A HOLE NEARBY.

LOOK BEFORE YOU LEAP.

Afterword

From as far back in time as we can tell, people everywhere have summed up their experiences and observations in short sayings, called *proverbs*, that can easily be remembered. Some proverbs go back many hundreds of years and are widely known around the world—for example, "Let sleeping dogs lie." Many use animal imagery to comment on human behavior. The proverb "If you live on a river, make friends with the crocodile" comes from India, where crocodiles are common, while "Even a monkey can fall out of a tree" comes from Japan, a country where monkeys live. The Nigerian proverb "When a mouse laughs at a cat, there is a hole nearby" could have been invented almost anywhere, of course. On the other hand, the proverb

"A leopard cannot change its spots," while familiar in the United States, had its origin in the Old Testament. And yet, even though tigers are not native to North America, the proverb "When you ride a tiger, you should not get off" originated in the US as a warning to act cautiously in a dangerous situation. Then there's the Mexican proverb "Don't check the teeth of a gift horse," which is a version of the well-known English proverb "Don't look a gift horse in the mouth." Both have a common root in medieval Latin. Speaking of horses, there is also this sound advice from no one knows where: "Don't ride two horses at the same time."

It is not surprising that proverbs— which are themselves verbal pictures—

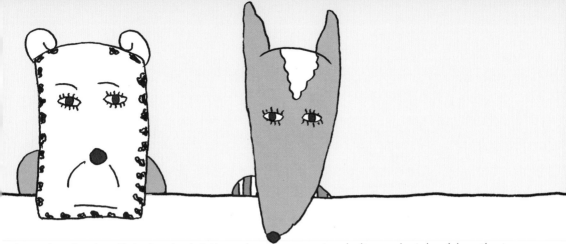

have inspired artists to depict them in woodcuts, drawings, paintings, cartoons, and on cups, plates, and plaques as well as T-shirts. For such common English-language proverbs as "Many hands make light work" and "A bad carpenter blames his tools," real-life situations can be imagined and turned into an illustration. Other proverbs direct us more broadly toward a safe and responsible life—"If you play with fire you will get burned" and "Look before you leap." There are even those stern proverbs that declare what is not possible in life or what should never be done: "You can't eat your cake and have it too," "Don't cry over spilled milk," and "Don't bite off more than you can chew." The European proverb "The pen is mightier than the sword" is more complex in its underlying idea that words are more powerful than brute force. And yet proverbs can also express their wisdom in a humorous fashion, as in "If you walk on thin ice, you might as well dance," which must come from some wintry place or other.

The proverb "Time you enjoy wasting is not wasted time" is interesting because it was coined only a century ago. This shows that not all proverbs are ancient and that modern life continues to hatch new proverbial wisdom. Lucky us to have these lively, appealing sayings we can use to salt our everyday writing and conversation. The perfect proverb is never out of season.

–Wolfgang Mieder
Professor Emeritus, University of Vermont

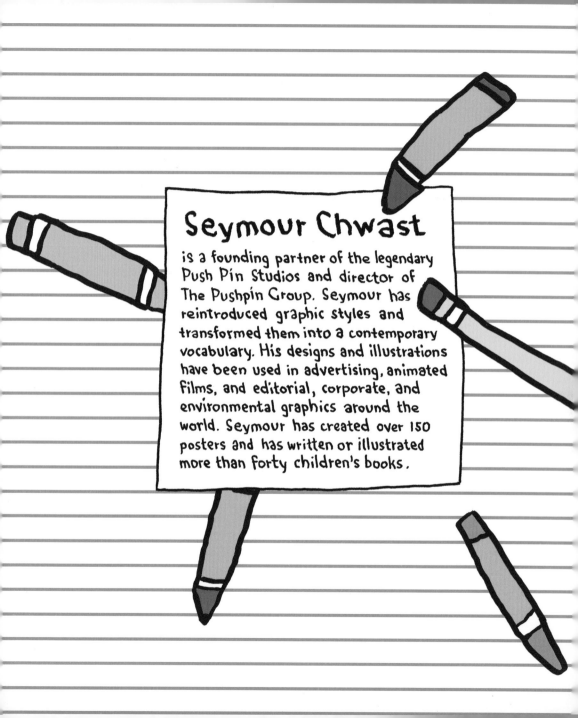

Seymour Chwast

is a founding partner of the legendary Push Pin Studios and director of The Pushpin Group. Seymour has reintroduced graphic styles and transformed them into a contemporary vocabulary. His designs and illustrations have been used in advertising, animated films, and editorial, corporate, and environmental graphics around the world. Seymour has created over 150 posters and has written or illustrated more than forty children's books.